A CASE STUDY IN COMMUNITY ORGANIZING

LESSONS FROM ONE CAMPAIGN FOR GAME-CHANGING SCHOOL REFORM

RAYMOND DOMANICO

FOREWORD BY MICHAEL GECAN

LESSONS FROM ONE CAMPAIGN FOR
GAME-CHANGING SCHOOL REFORM
Raymond Domanico
Foreword by Michael Gecan

Editing by Gregory F. Augustine Pierce
Cover and text design and typesetting by Andrea Reider

Text copyright © 2024 by Raymond Domanico
Foreword copyright © 2024 by Michael Gecan
Published by ACTA Publications, 7135 W. Keeney Street,
Niles, IL 60714, (800) 397-2282, www.actapublications.com

All rights reserved. No part of this publication may be reproduced or transmitted in any form or by any means, electronic or mechanical, including photocopying and recording, or by any information storage and retrieval system, including the Internet, without permission from the publisher. Permission is hereby given to use short excerpts with proper citation in reviews and marketing copy, church bulletins and handouts, and scholarly papers.

ISBN: 978-0-87946-731-9
Printed in the United States of America
by Total Printing Systems
Year 30 29 28 27 26 25 24 24
Printing 10 9 8 7 6 5 4 3 2 First
Text printed on 30% post-consumer recycled paper

FOREWORD
by Michael Gecan

If you read one piece—essay, pamphlet, study, or book—about education in American today, do yourself a favor and read this case study by educational analyst and chronicler Raymond Domanico. It has the advantage of a few years of time that has passed since the events chronicled here, but it is as relevant today as yesterday's news headlines.

Mr. Domanico worked with and for the leaders of Metro Industrial Areas Foundation in New York City for many years. Our clergy and lay leaders in East Brooklyn, the South Bronx, Queens, and Manhattan were trying to figure out how to engage with an educational monolith that served more than one million students, employed scores of thousands, squandered financial and social capital on bankrupt so-called local community school boards and an inert central bureaucracy that would make Charles Dickens quail. We realized we needed the assistance of someone who could provide the analysis of and perspective on New York's school system that we simply lacked. At the time we engaged with him, Ray had worked for the New York City Board of Education as a research professional and also written several perceptive studies of the system's limitations from his perch in a think tank. He turned out to be an ally we could trust, which is one of the lessons of this booklet.

From the start, Ray did what most experts fail to do. He recognized the essential role played by parents and community leaders in making meaningful change in education. He listened long and hard to the stories those leaders told about their experiences in their local schools. He tailored his research in response to the questions and insights those leaders expressed. And he respected the process of building meaningful public relationships within each local community as well as with allies and potential partners.

He did all this without using unnecessarily complicated academic terminology. There is no cant or ideology here. In the parlance of baseball, "see the ball; hit the ball." Don't overcomplicate things. Focus on the core reality of each situation. Ray saw the facts and teed up things so that parents, students, organizers, and community leaders could take a whack at specific improvements in primary and high school education that almost no one thought possible when we began.

I won't spoil your reading experience by summarizing the many pertinent-to-today observations and lessons that Ray cogently lays out in these pages. But I promise that the hour or two you need to read this piece, and perhaps discuss it with others, will be time very well spent—especially if you are as worried as I am about the future of education in our country and what organized people and their institutions can do about it.

LESSONS FROM ONE CAMPAIGN

Mike Gecan is the former co-executive director of the Industrial Areas Foundation (IAF) and the co-founder of Metro IAF, which operates east of the Mississippi River. He is the author of *Going Public: An Organizer's Guide to Citizens' Action, People's Institutions in Decline: Causes, Consequences, Cures,* and *Effective Organizing for Congregational Renewal.*

INTRODUCTION

Five Lessons for Public Engagement

I am not a community organizer. I am a 68-year-old educational researcher.

This is a book of lessons I learned from my experience fighting for and then supporting meaningful improvement in public schools in Brooklyn and the Bronx, New York City, from 1994-2010.

Here is what I think is still applicable to a wide and diverse communities, situations, and educational issues today:

1. Experts think about trends and systems, but people and relationships matter. Believe what you see with your own eyes.
2. Think big and ask for big things, but be ready to accept less. Know when to ask

publicly and when to ask privately. Always be intentional about the choice between fighting the system and working within it to achieve your goals.
3. Large institutions are resistant to change, but there are good people in them; you must cultivate those relationships.
4. Allies outside the educational system are important, particularly in complex issue areas. It does not matter if you do not agree on everything. However, I also learned the importance of protecting your own organizational identity.
5. Today's reforms or improvements will not last forever, you must stay in the game.

My Manhattan Institute Issue Brief, *The Transformation of Public High Schools in New York City,* on which this booklet is based, presented the facts and figures around New York's high school transformation; but the story of how and why this transformation came about and the unique array

INTRODUCTION

of individuals and organizations that drove the change is equally important.

What follows are stories of five lessons for public engagement and action that I believe are clear and still relevant from our successful organizing effort in New York City more than a decade ago.

Raymond Domanico
Senior Fellow & Director, Education Policy
Manhattan Institute
New York City
January 1, 2024

THE BACKSTORY

Good Intentions Are Never Enough

This is a short case study about how residents in the nation's largest city identified and labeled an issue of significant importance—the low quality of public schools in many neighborhoods—and organized themselves to engage with, fight as necessary, and then cooperate with public officials to change that system in meaningful ways.

This work was informed by thousands of individual and small group meetings with community residents. There was a widely held perception that the local schools were not delivering the quality of schooling that their community's children deserved and that the (pre-2001) leadership of the school system seemed unable or unwilling to change that awful dynamic.

Beyond the issue of low school performance, my colleagues and the community residents that we served also had to challenge the more widespread and accepted narratives about how change occurs in public schools. Among these was the notion that only heroic figures could improve inner city schools, a view that was very popular among some journalists and filmmakers of the time. Another was the notion that public schools could only improve when they were well/better funded, despite evidence that spending money wisely was more important than simply spending more money.

Other popular themes of the day included the idea that simply creating one well-functioning inner-city school as a model would somehow create a larger revolution in education circles. Finally, some believed that *only* teachers, or *only* parents, or *only* corporations, or only rich *foundations* could change schools for the better. Our work in New York City in the 2000s and 2010s was grounded in the belief that good schooling required the engagement of all those groups, and

THE BACKSTORY

more, all working together to create objectively better schools.

In 1997, I put a name to the school failure problem in a public report labeling over 40% of the city's local school districts "Educational Dead Zones." Their achievement results documented that in these districts there were no schools with acceptable test scores. Especially families in majority Black and Hispanic districts had few choices available to them other than the city's tuition-charging Catholic parochial schools or the few public schools in other neighborhoods with available seats that would accept students from outside their own districts. (For those families who could afford the tuition or whose children were lucky enough to get their tuition paid by groups of generous donors in the city, the Catholic schools were a lifeline. But there were many more children of color stuck in public schools that were simply not adequate.)

It was this reality that led the leaders and community organizers in East Brooklyn Congregations

(EBC), whom I knew at the time but with whom I was not yet formally affiliated, to act. In trying to understand how they might address the problem effectively, they sought to identify where there was a high overlap between the local public schools and the families in the local institutions and churches that were members of EBC. They found that in their corner of Brooklyn (roughly bordered by Williamsburg to the north, Jamaica Bay to the south, the Queens border on the east, and Prospect Park on the west), an area well served by subway and bus transit, many of the members of the local churches and other groups were sending their own children out of neighborhood to higher performing schools in the city's central business districts or in other nearby communities. This demonstrated the lengths to which parents were going to get their children a decent education, but it also made the task of organizing to solve the problem much more difficult, given the dispersion of their members' children across many schools.

This problem was not unique to Brooklyn or to New York City. By the second half of the twentieth century, low achievement of students from Black, Hispanic, and lower-income families had become endemic in many urban school systems.

THE BACKSTORY

In response, those school systems built up a wall of excuses to justify those outcomes, rather than addressing them head-on. This is not to say that the job of education was easy or that educators were universally uncaring, but there was a cottage industry of excuse-makers and rationalizers to be found. In our case, the City of New York had a major financial breakdown in the 1970s, and the impact of teacher layoffs and other budget cuts of that era were still felt in the decades that followed. But by the 1990s, money had begun to flow, programs were beginning to be restored, and poorly maintained school buildings were being repaired or replaced. In the educational dead zones, however, way too many kids were still being left far behind.

A big part of the problem was that good intentions were not enough. The things most observers could see and control "downtown," at New York Public Schools (NYPS) headquarters, were not the things that really needed to be changed to improve outcomes in the schools. I had spent the first few years of my career working in the central headquarters of the school system as a data analyst and researcher. When I was evaluating programs that centrally designed and funded programs that were then shipped out to schools as a set of rules and regulations, the results were consistent: The (whatever) program enjoyed modest success (or failure); but also, the results varied widely across individual schools. Researchers in other cities across the country noticed the same thing, and the awareness grew that the actual schools mattered more than the programs they offered.

It turned out that schools are more complex than they look from afar. Their success depends upon a complicated mix of critical relationships between teachers and students, among the adults in the school, and between the school and families. To crack the nut of school failure and actually improve the schools, people had to take a deep look at the individual schools, not a superficial look at their statistics. Much of what is described in the coming pages is about getting to that point.

In the end, the solution to the widespread school failure looked different in different schools across the city. Over the years, many groups learned to set aside their differences with one another and work towards the common good, including the creation

THE BACKSTORY

of a diverse set of better schools representing different approaches and methods but all pointing at better schooling for the city's least-well-served communities.

While this story is about the transformation of New York City's public high schools between 1994 and 2014, the lessons of this effort are applicable to other areas of public service and community life. Much of what follows details the work of the Industrial Areas Foundation-Metro New York and its affiliates, East Brooklyn Congregations (EBC) and South Bronx Churches (SBC), each of which designed and established new public high schools in New York City in ways I will describe. I was an educational research advisor to these two organizations from 1999 to 2010.

Other groups in New York at the time approached the school's problem in ways quite different from ours, and that diversity of approaches proved to be key to the success of the various efforts. The important commonality was to create educational opportunity in previously underserved communities. That was something that the system had failed to do for generations. Community organizations like ours, as well as committed educators within the failing system, had the will and the expertise to take on the educational mission that the old system had abandoned, but they needed to be occasionally encouraged and always supported in their fight against their own bureaucracy.

Eventually, the system itself was transformed by a combination of external and internal pressure, followed by enlightened leadership that adopted the approach of the local reformers. In the end, the city's entire high school system had been overhauled and greater access to good schools at all levels, elementary, middle, and high schools had been established. Though this effort did not produce miracles, it succeeded where previous and more recent efforts have failed. This decade-long, sustained effort offers insight into ways that challenge those who see education as a conflict between warring factions as opposed to a partnership among educators, communities, and families.

East Brooklyn Congregations and South Bronx Churches participated in the overhaul of their city's public schools from the beginning in the hands-on way that is described here. Early in their schools campaigns, EBC and SBC learned that advocacy was not enough. The situation in their local public high schools was so dire and the system at the time was so unresponsive that these groups had to take the remarkable step of opening their own public high schools. They needed to directly challenge the organizational orthodoxy that had stubbornly maintained the approach to high school education which emerged in the middle years of the twentieth century: Traditional high schools were large and departmentalized, organized around academic subjects. By the late twentieth century, particularly in urban areas, this approach was failing, with fewer than half the students earning high school diplomas. The smaller, more personalized high schools that were created in New York City between 1994 and 2014 produced significantly better outcomes for students, particularly Black and Hispanic residents of the city's poorer neighborhoods.

LESSON ONE

Believe What You See with Your Own Eyes

Education is not easy. One thing that makes it complicated is that, while learning occurs through a series of very local and immediate relationships, those relationships have typically been governed from afar: by the legislature, courts, professional organizations, or bureaucracies. For almost seventy years, since the Supreme Court struck down the existence of state-sanctioned school segregation in Brown vs. Board of Education in 1954, America's states and cities have grappled with the difficulty of providing high quality schools to all our residents, regardless of race. That is tragically ironic, since the highest court in the land ordered states with racially separate public-school systems to end that practice "with all deliberate speed." Eventually, the southern states with legally sanctioned school segregation did take those laws off the books, but segregation and the relegation of low-income children of color to inferior schools proved to require more than simply changing the law.

New York City, where I have worked on education policy for over 40 years, went through many failed attempts to bring about wide-spread integration or improvement in its schools. From the 1950s through the mid-1960s, the city made half-hearted attempts to desegregate schools by moving students around to better improve the racial mix in individual schools. As in the rest of the county, many white parents rallied around the concept of neighborhood schools in opposition to integration efforts. The city's Black and Hispanic (in those days, mostly Puerto-Rican) communities embraced what they called "community control" of schools, as the city could not seem to achieve integration. Meanwhile, the teachers in the city were building a single city-wide union.

LESSON ONE

These movements all clashed, leading to intense racial division and a series of teacher strikes in the late 1960s. A hybrid school system of thirty-two local school districts emerged, with elected school boards holding limited power. Those boards could hire the principals for their schools, but they could only hire teachers from lists of teachers who were approved by the central headquarters. In a major concession to the newly powerful teachers' union, the local boards could not fire teachers, or principals, without going through a lengthy and often unsuccessful arbitration process. Meanwhile, as was occurring in many parts of the country, parents and others with the means were leaving the city for the surrounding suburbs and their shiny new, well-run, and racially and economically isolated public schools. The city school system was becoming a majority-minority institution and would face a crippling financial crisis in the mid-1970s as New York City flirted with bankruptcy.

The attitudes and practices formed in these years of racial conflict, financial stress, and aggressive labor-management conflict set the atmosphere that ruled and paralyzed the school system for decades while far too many children were failing. That finally began to change in the mid-to-late 1990s in ways I will describe in this case study. What is important to know at the outset is that the success that New York City finally found did not come from any single planned methodology. Many people and organizations can honestly say they participated in getting this movement started, but they were not coordinating their efforts; in fact, many of them disagreed with each other rather strongly. My former colleague, Mike Gecan, has pointed out that other major changes in New York City's public safety, housing, and public transportation came about in similar ways to this education effort—with different groups setting aside their differences to work towards a common goal.

One high school in the South Bronx tells the story of the rise and fall of urban public education. The Morris High School building, sitting on a high hill in the Bronx, embodies the lofty dream of public secondary education at its dawn in the nineteenth century, the nightmare that was inner-city secondary education in the late decades of the

LESSON ONE

twentieth century, and the small revival that began in the first years of the twenty-first century. Morris was the first public high school in the Bronx and the city's first co-educational high school. It opened in 1897 and its purpose was clear—to provide immigrant and working-class students with a college preparatory education. Its building, designed in the gothic style and overlooking the surrounding area, reinforced this mission, and today that building appears on the National Register of Historic Places. At its peak, Morris High enrolled over 4,000 students, but it eventually became a factory of failure, and its final graduating class in 2005 included only one hundred students.

The growth and the decline of Morris High School were emblematic of the evolution of urban secondary education over the course of the twentieth century. Founded in the earliest days of public secondary education, Morris was meant to serve a small slice of the population, those students considered capable of academic learning as preparation for college. As public high schools became more common and popular, they opened to all students, changed their goals, broadened their curriculum, and became more standardized in their approach. By mid-twentieth-century, the

LESSONS FROM ONE CAMPAIGN

creation of professional standards and practices, teacher licensing, and expansion of the age of compulsory education had solidified the place of the large, comprehensive high schools designed to serve both the college-bound and those destined to directly enter the workforce upon graduation. That type of school remains the norm in school districts across the country today. They work in many places but, in the poorest urban areas, large comprehensive high schools found themselves being asked by state authorities to prepare most or all students for college at a time when many families with the inclination and social capital needed to send their children to college were abandoning the urban schools for those in the suburbs. Many urban high schools saw their demographics change dramatically, eventually serving almost exclusively Black, Puerto Rican, and other Hispanic students.

Urban public high schools like Morris found themselves on the wrong side of a shift in the expectations laid upon all high schools. As the late sociologist Martin Trow, my advisor in graduate school, observed: "When few students went on to college, there was no disgrace in not doing so; moreover, except for the professions it was not so clear that occupational success was closely linked to academic achievement." Noting that "...the transformation from not going to college into failure [in life] has both social and psychological consequences," Professor Trow went on. "The more the high school is organized around the college preparatory programs," he said, "and the more it stresses academic achievement, the more punishing it will be for the non-achievers."

By the mid-1970s, two-thirds of all students in the city's public schools were Black or Hispanic. While the city was still offering academically challenging programs in its most selective high schools, as well as in its neighborhood academic and magnet high schools in the less poor (and less white) areas, the unstated goal of *college prep for most if not all* was never achieved in much of the city.

All the stresses described by Trow were evident in the New York City public high school system in the 1970s, 1980s, and early 1990s and were exacerbated by the widespread separation of the achievers and non-achievers into different schools. The non-achievers, including some who might have been achievers in better schools, were lumped into large "dropout factories" and considered failures.

LESSONS FROM ONE CAMPAIGN

A 1978 study by the *New York Times* described the New York City's public high school system at the time as serving over 380,000 students in one hundred high schools (seventy-eight "Competitive or Academic/Comprehensive" and twenty-two "Vocational-Technical"). This story noted that "During the late 1960s and early 1970s, high schools across the country broadened their curriculum offerings as means of making education relevant to students and encouraging potential dropouts to stay in school." It also reported that "this year's [1975] high school seniors have taken far more remedial, modified, or otherwise watered-down courses in all of the basic academic areas than their counterparts in the class of 1973." This development was occurring just as the Board of Education was planning to "upgrade the standards for high school graduation, which would require students to read at least at the ninth-grade level and perform arithmetic computations at the eighth-grade level to receive their diplomas."

In fact, the city's traditional high school system, comprised of those one hundred or so high

LESSON ONE

schools for decades, failed not only at college prep for all (or even most) but also at being a universally successful "terminal" program. The Board of Education's 1973 goal was to upgrade standards to eighth-grade level in math and ninth-grade in reading. In 1987, while employed at the school system, I completed the first longitudinal study of students from entry to high school through the next four years through the city's school system. That report found that forty-one percent of the students who first entered high school in fall of 1982 had earned either a high school diploma or equivalency by June 1986. Subsequent administrations modified the analysis slightly to remove the twelve percent of students who had left the city system for other schools during high school. This then re-calculated the graduation rate as 46.5%. It remained close to that level for the next sixteen years. By 2002, still only 50.8% of city public high school students graduated in the expected four years. Even with its low expectations, at the end of the 20th century, the largest public high school system in the country was attaining a standard of success that had been originally set back in the 1950s as a *minimal* national goal: high school graduation for one-half of its students!

LESSONS FROM ONE CAMPAIGN

If the nation's largest school system looked terrible from the bird's-eye view of the experts and analysts, it looked far starker to parents and others struggling to get their kids through a system in which most of the kids in their neighborhoods did not get through high school unscathed. While there were ample examples of heroic educators fighting the good fight, the general built-in apathy of the entire system to the academic success of students from lower income families often beat back their valiant attempts.

The efforts of the organizers and leaders of East Brooklyn Congregations (EBC) to work with the school system to change the trajectory above illuminate the problem. EBC had garnered a good amount of public recognition with their Nehemiah Homes, a bold initiative that built whole communities of working-class families in areas that the city leaders had deemed worthy of abandonment, a policy often referred to as "planned shrinkage." Following their historic housing efforts, the EBC turned their attention to the problem of public education in those newly built communities,

LESSON ONE

where the local public high schools were graduating fewer students than were dropping out. They crafted a response, titled "Nehemiah II," through which they garnered promises from local employers, including banks, public utilities, and private business to guarantee an entry-level job to any student who graduated from local high schools.

The program went further than that, with EBC volunteers tutoring and mentoring students in these schools. When graduation time came for the first group of students to go all the way through this program, many did not get the promised jobs because they failed to meet basic competency tests required by the potential employers.

It was soon after this that I was introduced to EBC and the Industrial Areas Foundation (IAF) by a foundation executive who was funding the work of my colleagues and me at the market-oriented Manhattan Institute for Policy Research. It was a strange partnership for EBC, but their lead organizer at the time, Dave Nelson, nonetheless proceeded and met with us educational researchers in 1990 to describe what had happened with their Nehemiah II educational efforts. My colleagues and I were pushing a novel idea at the time: stop trying to fix failing and non-responsive schools;

create new ones to replace them. We offered to work with EBC's leaders on the design of a new, smaller, and more personalized local public high school, which they could then present to the city's Board of Education for approval.

We worked well together; eventually EBC had a proposal, drafted by a former New York City public high school principal, Lew Smith, for two small public high schools to educate about 500 students each. These would be part of "the public-school system," with EBC serving in a sponsoring/partnering role. Part of the plan was to require the Board of Education to include EBC in the selection process for the principals of these schools. Board of Education educators had been creating these types of non-traditional schools in small numbers, but EBC's proposal was the first one developed and presented by a powerful, grassroots, community organization. That in itself was a great challenge to the school system, which had worked hard to keep "the community" at bay for decades.

EBC would eventually see their two schools open in 1992, but only after tragedy (described in a later section) forced the Board of Education's hand.

LESSON TWO

Ask for Big Things, Be Ready to Accept Less

As **I have described,** the leaders of East Brooklyn Congregations had spent several years pushing for the reform of two local, and failing, high schools: Thomas Jefferson and Bushwick. Disappointed with the system's inability to improve those schools and encouraged by the ideas that some of my colleagues at the time suggested to them, they eventually produced the notion of proposing two new small high schools as alternatives to the failing schools. A similar effort was undertaken by the IAF affiliate in the South Bronx, South Bronx Churches (SBC). While educators had been allowed to create a small number of new schools within the system before, the notion of community involvement in school creation and implementation was a red flag to the leadership of the school system.

In the mid-to-late 1960s in New York City, leaders in the city's Black and later Puerto Rican communities were fed-up with the system's inability or unwillingness to make much progress on the #1 civil rights issue of the day—racial integration of the schools. This led them to embrace the concept of community control of the schools—breaking up the nation's largest school district into smaller districts with their own school boards and superintendents. Given the residential segregation of the city, this would lead many of the non-white areas to have their own school district and control thereof.

Battles over community control, particularly how it would apply to the hiring and firing of teachers, sparked two long and contentious teacher strikes in the late sixties. The fights over this issue split two major democratic constituencies in the city: teachers and their supporters and the Black and Puerto Rican communities. An uneasy peace was forged in 1970 with the adoption of a watered-down form of community control, with budgets and hiring remaining in the hands of the central Board of Education and the local boards having

LESSON TWO

limited powers. A good number, maybe a third of these boards, eventually became captured by political interests more concerned with jobs and contracts than educational quality. In 1989, leaders of the IAF-affiliated organizations in New York City called for the elimination of these boards in a joint op-ed entitled "Drain the School Swamp." Despite the apathy of many in the city about the failure of school boards and of the central Board of Education to do anything about real change in the system, the proposal to start new high schools with different rules struck a nerve in some veterans of a system that was using a then twenty-year-old conflict to resist all efforts to give community leaders any real involvement in their children's schools.

Although the proposals made by EBC and SBC were getting nominal support from the leadership of the school system at the time, there seemed to be foot-dragging going on, voiced in terms of the "delicacy of the situation." Then tragedy intervened.

On February 27, 1992, two students, Ian More and Tyrone Sinkler, were tragically shot and killed inside Thomas Jefferson High School, only an hour before a scheduled visit by then New York City Mayor David Dinkins. Both boys had funerals at congregations that were members of East Brooklyn Congregations. Shortly after the funerals, the schools chancellor agreed to sit down with East Brooklyn Congregations' leaders to discuss their plan for new schools. They told EBC that they would support the opening of their two new schools. That effort eventually grew to include a new school proposed by South Bronx Churches and new schools proposed by several other groups in the city. It was aided by the receipt of a $25 million grant from the Annenberg Foundation to the organization now known as New Visions as part of the $500 million "Annenberg Challenge to Improve America's Schools."

After the planning and identification of buildings that could house new schools, a group of new high schools opened in 1996. Today, in 2023, thirty-seven high schools that opened in 1996 remain in operation in the city school system. After those openings, twenty-five additional small high schools in operation today opened in 1999, and an additional twenty-two opened in 2001, with a handful of others also opening in the other years between 1996 and 2001.

LESSON TWO

In this case, the IAF affiliate organizations' request for the creation of new schools was small in reach but bold in concept, running against the defensive culture of the school system. In a short time, however, its reach extended as the school system agreed with many other groups in the city on the creation of their own new schools.

Eight years after the opening of the two EBC high schools in Brooklyn and the South Bronx's Bronx Leadership Academy (BLA), the IAF organizations returned with another big ask. Having just opened Bronx Leadership Academy II, which built on the success of the original BLA, leaders of South Bronx Churches approached the schools chancellor with a proposal to have the city alleviate school overcrowding in the Bronx through the construction of a multi-school campus on land that had long housed a vacant train yard. Their proposal was for a seven-school campus. SBC had engaged architect Alexander Gorlin to do a broad sketch of the proposal, and he provided us with a three-dimensional cardboard model of the plan. Our organizers prepared all of us who would attend the meeting with the chancellor. Most of the discussion would be led by the volunteer leaders, with a few of us staff in attendance to speak up if anything went off the rails. Each team member had their assigned topics to pitch, and all were prepared to answer any question we anticipated might come from the chancellor or his staff.

We arrived at the school system's headquarters in the 1890-era "Tweed Courthouse" in downtown Manhattan, carrying our cardboard model of the new campus, and had one last walk-through before being ushered into a conference room to meet with Joel Klein, then schools chancellor of the New York City public school system. Our leaders started speaking, each hitting all the right notes as the chancellor looked intently at the model. We didn't get to finish our pitch. Less than fifteen minutes into the presentation, Klein said, "I like it, I just have to get the mayor on board, give me a few weeks."

Now, in the world of sales or fundraising, a general rule is that when they say yes, you thank them and leave the room. In other words, don't mess it up once you have the agreement. So that's what we did. We thanked Klein and, in a bit of a collective haze, walked out to the front steps of Tweed and did our post-meeting evaluation. "What just happened?" was the first reaction. We were asking the city to commit over $100 million to a school construction project, and we got a yes. Was that real? We knew Klein but, seriously, this was a big ask. (The reaction was a 180-degree turnaround from the time a few years earlier when local school board in the Bushwick section of Brooklyn publicly called EBC an "illegitimate parent organization" because it had the audacity to publicly call them out on their failing schools.)

We *trusted,* we *celebrated,* but we continued to *monitor* the situation. Things moved quickly, but it took a bit longer than a few weeks. We were eventually told they would build four schools, not seven, which was fine with us. The four school buildings would serve over 2,000 students in state-of-the-art facilities, and the project would eventually cost close to $250 million dollars—the most expensive school construction project in the city's history. Our only concern was that the commitment made to us had still not been made public. Finally, on very short notice, we were asked to attend a press

LESSONS FROM ONE CAMPAIGN

conference in South Bronx High School at which the mayor would speak and announce the project publicly. It was all very hurried at the end, and no one asked us to bring some leaders to speak at the event. We worried that our role might be downplayed; that happens in politics. Again, we liked Schools Chancellor Klein, but it was best to be prepared. We wrote up a brief but pointed press release of our own, making clear that this project had been proposed by South Bronx Churches. I had about 50 copies of it in my brief case when we went to the event. They never came out. As soon as we arrived in the auditorium, the mayor's and chancellor's aides asked us to have two of SBC's leaders join the mayor on stage and say a few words, so Virginia Gonzalez, a life-long resident of the South Bronx and leader in SBC, joined in the program with the Mayor Bloomberg, describing SBC's work to bring about this new campus.

The lessons we had already learned were: Know when to ask publicly or privately, and always be intentional about the choice between fighting the system and working with it to achieve your goals.

LESSON THREE

Large Institutions Are Resistant, But Some Good People Work There

By the 1990s, the graduation numbers had made it clear to many that something dramatic needed to be done with the public high school system in New York City. The pressure for change and various designs for new approaches to secondary education emerged from school-level educators inside the system and from community members outside.

The city's public education system had long included dedicated teachers who had chafed under the strict bureaucratic dictates of the hierarchical school system. These were largely educators who considered themselves progressive in pedagogical terms; that is, they favored a *constructivist* approach to teaching and learning. This approach placed the classroom teacher in the role of *facilitator* of the student's learning as opposed to the *transmitter* of educational content and knowledge. Students are then encouraged and expected to pursue their own path to the subject matter, think critically about it, and arrive at knowledge through this process. As a *City Journal* article by Seymour Fliegel, "Debbie Meier and the Dawn of Central Park East: When Teachers Take Charge of Schooling" put it at the time: "Instead of having the students relying on someone else's information and accepting it as truth, the students should be exposed to data, primary sources, and the ability to interact with other students so that they can learn from the incorporation of their experiences."

One high school of this type was organized around the following principles: *that less is more; that it is better to know some things well than to attempt to cover many things superficially; that high standards must be set for all students; that students demonstrate mastery of their subjects through exhibitions and portfolios; that teaching and learning must be personalized; that students are perceived as workers and teachers as coaches; and, finally, that youngsters discover answers and solutions to problems by being active learners.*

In the 1980s and 1990s, the system had allowed the creation of some high schools that followed the constructivist approach; but these largely served special populations from second-chance schools for students who had fallen severely behind or who were returning to school at a new International High School for recent immigrants after having dropped out. One school district in the city, District 4 in East Harlem, had also supported the MacArthur-award-winning educator Deborah Meier, who founded Central Park East elementary school, which eventually grew to include a middle school and a high school, all using the constructivist approach. These schools became a proving ground for young teachers who believed in this philosophy and, as many traditional high schools in the system seemed stuck at low levels of performance, these educators began to clamor for more opportunities to show that their approach could succeed where the traditional system had failed.

LESSONS FROM ONE CAMPAIGN

A fair amount of energy was dedicated to the debate between progressive educators, who had their vision of a new pedagogy, and more traditional-leaning community groups who simply wanted better schools. Left unsaid in these debates was the understanding that New York City's public high schools were caught in the grip of a century-long nationwide evolution in the purpose and scope of secondary education. By the 1960s, that process had left many high schools in urban centers across the country left out in a game of musical chairs that was not of their making. By the 1990s, Morris High School was one of many public high schools in the city that appeared to most as so-called "dropout factories," with the number of dropouts far outpacing the number of graduates.

Work rules in the city system shielded principals from any responsibility for school performance. Once granted tenure, principals were guaranteed they would remain at the helm of a particular school unless they violated laws, engaged in gross misconduct, or retired. Combined with the similar protections for tenured teachers, these rules almost ensured that the process of high

LESSON THREE

schooling would go on year in and year out without any real regard to student outcomes. Liberals and conservatives alike railed against the rules and the unrelenting levels of student failure, but few educators honestly or publicly considered the larger transformation that had occurred in American secondary education and the precarious place that urban high schools had been placed. Any change suggested from the outside in this system that asked high school educators to accomplish much more with a broader segment of their students may well have spurred the growth of educational workers unions and the many protections they sought in New York City, and these unions were often viewed by community organizations and others as impediments to reform.

As the Annenberg Challenge money dried up at the end of the century and the leadership of the NYC school system turned over, the notion of starting new high schools ceased to have the support of the school system. This changed in early 2001, when a new philanthropic effort, led by the Gates Foundation, solicited ideas for a high school improvement effort on a large scale. At the time, I was working with organizations that were members of the Metro Industrial Areas Foundation, particularly South Bronx Churches and East Brooklyn Congregations. South Bronx Churches was asked by the Bronx Superintendent of High Schools, Norman Wechsler, to partner with his office in seeking a grant from Gates to transform high schools in the borough, beginning with the closure of Morris High School and the development of four new small high schools to occupy the huge Morris High building.

Our group had caught the eye of the superintendent because in the mid-1990s they had successfully pushed the Board of Education to create a new small high school, Bronx Leadership Academy in the South Bronx in response to the low level of performance of Morris and other public high schools in the area. The new school struggled at first but hit its stride under the inspired leadership of principal Katherine Kelly. By the year 2000, it had garnered a reputation for producing high results and for being a training ground for emerging school leaders among its faculty, several which went on to lead other high schools in the borough over the years. When Superintendent Weschler

LESSON THREE

wanted to show representatives of the Gates foundation that change in support of better education for the children of the South Bronx was possible, he brought them to Bronx Leadership Academy.

South Bronx Churches was not alone in this community-led effort to revive successful secondary education in the city's poorer neighborhoods. The 2001 effort of the Bronx Superintendent and South Bronx Churches (SBC) was funded by a grant from the Gates Foundation and coordinated in the city by the non-profit New Visions for Public Schools, who had also coordinated the earlier Annenberg Challenge in the city. The role assigned to South Bronx Churches was to recruit community partners to work with the teams of educators in the design of the new schools. This collaboration was a condition of the grant from Gates. The community partners were meant, in some cases, to provide additional services to students in the new schools and, in other cases, to provide the new schools with an anchor in the communities they were meant to serve. (This was partially intended to provide the schools with a community ally who might be able to keep the larger system at bay.)

The task of recruiting local non-profits was complicated by the bad experiences that many had suffered in previous efforts to provide services in schools. These experiences took many forms, but they often came down to a simple sense that the community partners were not really a priority of the school. For example, groups with contracts to provide after-school services—which had expanded from recreation programs to include tutoring and other academic services—found that little information would be shared on a regular and transparent basis with them about specific client-students' particular needs. Eventually, my colleagues and I at South Bronx Churches, as well as project staff from the district office, were able to convince parents and local organizations that this effort would be different.

On the education front, the work of Bronx High School Deputy Superintendent Eric Nadelstern was crucial. He had been involved in earlier efforts of small-school creation, including the Annenberg Challenge, and had thought a lot about how to design successful new schools. In the Bronx in 2001, he designed and implemented a comprehensive process for prospective school designers (educators and community leaders) to be trained before submitting their proposals and

LESSON THREE

for independent community reviewers to evaluate those proposals and recommend which should go forward. This process was deliberative and intensive, including weekly training sessions in the Morris High School auditorium for community leaders and follow-up hands-on consultation with design teams by members of Nadelstern's staff. Each team had to formally present its final design plan to a committee of district leaders, representatives of the teachers' union, and other leading educators to gain approval to start their schools.

The Bronx initiative took off in earnest when it expanded across the city after the election of Mayor Michael Bloomberg and the appointment of Joel Klein as his schools chancellor. When Chancellor Klein decided to rapidly expand this effort to the other boroughs, he put Eric Nadelstern in charge of the effort and used his process in all five boroughs. Beginning in 2003, the city opened an average of 26 new Department of Education-administered small high schools a year for six straight years. (That effort continued until it was ended by Mayor Bill de Blasio in 2014; an additional 72 small DOE high schools had opened by then, 228 in all over 11 years.)

LESSONS FROM ONE CAMPAIGN

The efforts of innovative public-school teachers and concerned community groups in the 1990s and the courageous endorsement and expansion of this effort by the new mayor and his schools chancellor in the early 2000s was an inflection point in a long and torturous history of how larger national expectations placed on the country's public secondary schools affected urban areas.

As the Bloomberg administration took hold of the school system, having entered office in the middle of the 2001-02 school year, the graduation rate began a sustained and dramatic increase. As of 2020, the graduation rate was either 83 percent, using the city's historical measure, or 79 percent using the slightly different methodology introduced by the State of New York Education Department in 2008. That welcome improvement occurred as the city moved dramatically away from its static system of one hundred or so large high schools to a more differentiated and dynamic system of smaller high school creation and replacement in New York City.

In all these groundbreaking efforts, the Metro Industrial Areas Foundation affiliates found

LESSON THREE

themselves working with veteran educators who were members of the very system they had been fighting for so long. We found that in this case they were fighting the same battle from within that system. Those relationships delivered benefits for years. Katherine Kelly, the principal responsible for Bronx Leadership Academy's (BLA's) initial success, mentored not only her successor, Ken Gaskins, but his successor as well, Ivan Yipp, who started as a teacher in BLA. Another teacher who worked for Kelly, Paulette Franklin, was the founding principal of Bronx Leadership Academy II, as was her successor Elyse Doti. Doti was in turn succeeded by Katherine Callaghan, another teacher in the original BLA. In Brooklyn, a teacher and guidance counsellor in the EBC East New York high school (since closed), Catherine Reilly, designed and was the founding principal of the Bushwick Leaders High School for Academic Excellence.

Good public institutions, including good community organizations like EBC and SBC, develop their own future leaders. To do this, schools need to be intentional about developing future teachers and future school leaders. They also need the system to grant them flexibility in hiring, so that when former students appear with the proper education and credentials, they may hire them as teachers (as opposed to hiring the next person on a civil service list). Good schools also need to intentionally develop the leadership potential of their teachers, giving them opportunities to spend part of their time organizing with the community and running projects within the school's outreach programs; to spend time shadowing school leaders like principals and assistant principals; and encouraging them to mentor young teachers and get the professional licenses or certifications they need to be an education leader.

This intentional effort is critical, because education is a tough profession, and there is a tremendous amount of staff turnover. I've seen too many good schools fail when a new principal who did not understand the critical importance of a particular school's professional culture was chosen to replace a principal who "got" the connection between school culture and success but was now retiring or moving on in some other way.

Over the years, the Metro IAF affiliates also forged productive public relationships with numerous administrators and leaders in the city-wide school system. At first, they tended to be

LESSON THREE

administrators trying courageously to buck the system, such as Steve Phillips, the Superintendent of Alternative High Schools, who supported our first three high schools. Eric Nadelstern led the Gates-funded initiative in the Bronx, and we worked often with him as a community partner. When the system turned in our direction after the election of Mayor Michael Bloomberg, we forged a lasting and productive working relationship with Schools Chancellor Joel Klein and then Dennis Walcott. We didn't get everything we asked for, but we always got a fair hearing. In the construction of the Mott Haven Campus in the South Bronx and the Spring Creek Campus in East New York, first proposed by SBC and EBC respectively, Lorraine Grillo, head of the School Construction Authority and then First Deputy Mayor of New York City, was a supportive and responsive ally.

LESSON FOUR

You Have to Maintain Your Identity

When I first met East Brooklyn Congregations (EBC) in 1990, my organization, a market-oriented policy institute, was also trying to build relationships with a group of well-performing alternative public schools in the city. These schools were largely led by hard-working and committed educators who believed in trying to tap the inner creativity and inquisitiveness of their students rather than lecturing those students from a set and stoic curriculum. Within bounds, discussion and inquiry were valued more than the delivery of knowledge from teacher to student. Their schools were good and caring institutions, and their graduates went on to success in college, as they do to this day. The fact that a market-oriented policy group was attempting to work with progressive educators who were largely left-leaning in their own political views was an early indication that concerned people in New York were learning how to put aside their differences to work for improvement in education.

In my youthful exuberance, I thought I saw the opportunity for a coalition across political lines. But East Brooklyn Congregations (EBC) and South Bronx Churches (SBC) did not share in my enthusiasm. They were focused on getting new and better schools for the communities they served and were wary of formally associating with a city-wide group of progressive educators that offered a single vision of what schooling should look like across all communities. They were intent on maintaining their own vision, independence, and flexibility on a wide range of issues on which the Manhattan Institute had also staked its own positions. Each of the three groups had valid reasons for maintaining their independence, while sometimes collaborating. Today, after my stint with IAF, I am once again working at the Institute and continue to hold the progressive educators, now known as the New York Performance Standards Consortium in high regard.

LESSON FOUR

Taking time and effort to build a formal coalition would have been an unnecessary waste of time and effort. The lesson I learned was that people feel strongly about associating with like-minded people and avoiding those with generally contrary views, even when the groups agreed on a specific issue. The progressive educators, the IAF organizations, and the education team at the Manhattan Institute did share a common belief that New York City's Board of Education, as then organized, was an impediment to game-changing change and improvement. In a city like New York dominated by a single political party, in this case the Democrats, it is often difficult for people of one ideology or another to confront a huge public institution that is a major source of jobs and contracts in the city's public sphere. Our liberal friends were employees of that system, and while they could challenge that system from within, working with a group from a conservative think tank and community organizations that were not controlled by the system was a bridge too far for most of them.

Some of us met again in 2001, but a lot of things had changed since the earlier effort. First, I was

LESSONS FROM ONE CAMPAIGN

now working with Metro IAF in NYC as an education advisor. More importantly, both EBC and SBC had successfully launched two high schools which, according to a study from New York University, were punching above their weight—getting higher achievement from student bodies than their demographic profile would predict based on the current performance patterns in the school system. Some of the so-called "progressive" schools in the system also had impressive records, but they were still not getting the respect they deserved from the leadership of the school system.

A third group entered the mix in 2001, in response to the invitation from the Gates Foundation to re-imagine public high schools in the Bronx. In this project, prospective schools needed to have a community-based or non-profit partner. There were many fine, well-directed agencies in the city at that time, but there were also some clunkers, perhaps corrupted by the scramble for contracts and the political associations that were often required to secure those contracts. For many of the good groups that I met in the South Bronx in 2001, the impediment was that they previously had bad experiences partnering with the Board of

LESSON FOUR

Education and were unsure about diving into the issue of the creation of new public high schools. I assured them that entering the partnership with the Bronx High School District was a bit of a leap of faith for South Bronx Churches as well, but that we felt that we had built up our strength to the point where we could fight any battles that ensued. (I may have also implied that we would help them if it seemed that they were being compromised by the school system!)

In the years following this coalition's coming together in the South Bronx, we saw the city expand the high school creation effort across the entire city, as I have previously described. Those years were characterized by a relative peace among the good people and organizations of the city and its neighborhoods. Yes, we still could find areas of disagreement, but in an environment where the system itself had adopted the concepts of replacing low-performing schools with more promising ones, and with new friends in City Hall, it was not necessary or advisable to air those differences in public. Each group in this effort shared the same common goal of creating better schools for children in the city's poorer neighborhoods. It no longer mattered whose approaches were the best. Success mattered, and we learned that success could come from a variety of approaches.

Part of the lesson here was that the city's leadership in these years of educational renaissance were willing to open the design and sponsorship of public schools to *many* groups. The abundance of opportunity, as opposed to the previous scarcity of options by school officials who were more defensive in their approach, allowed for different partnerships to bloom. Under the old regime, community groups and non-profits understood there were only few open slots, and this bred the unhealthy conflict and competition that eventually proved to be unnecessary. Each group could pursue its own vision, within broad limits, without needing to argue that their approach was not only good but better than everyone else's.

In fact, the *avoiding of coalitions* can often carry a price. In our case, in the 1990s and 2000s, many well-intentioned philanthropic foundations saw the world in two dimensions—the "system" and the "community." They rightfully saw the system as large and powerful, but they underestimated the power of well-organized, relational community organizations. Their common plea was that the "good groups" in the community should band together to speak as one voice to the "oppressing system." That approach was simply not realistic.

The process of coalition building is difficult in and of itself. Maintaining that coalition often requires muting one's own beliefs in favor of a watered-down consensus. Ironically, our efforts in the Bronx and elsewhere mirrored part of what the foundations wanted: coalesce around a common, yet simple, vision of better schools of whatever philosophy, while avoiding the time-suck of endless and poorly-run meetings, deliberations, and consensus-building that formal coalitions require. Finally, it is often the case that coalitions form around single issues, like school funding, or single areas like education or housing. IAF-affiliated organizations, on the other hand, all operate in multiple-issue areas at once, and this proves to be a great advantage when cultivating productive public relationships with officeholders and public and private officials who can help change things.

For example, there were times when a mayor or a governor or a bureaucrat—or a bank president or small-business owner or investor or foundation head—were assumed to be out-of-step with our views on education, but we found we could work with them on other issues of importance and then, perhaps, engage them on a particular aspect of education. Rather than trying to engage potential allies solely on education, we would use other issues to develop our leaders, hone their ideas, bring new institutions into the organization—all while waiting for the political moment to press our educational agenda.

LESSON FIVE

Today's Win Will Not Last Forever

Of the 485 district-run and charter high schools in operation in New York City as of 2021, 425 were created between 1994 and 2014, and these new schools were now educating two-thirds of the city's high school students. What did all this radical (as in "root cause") accomplish? What was learned from New York City's high school reform projects of the late 1990s, 2000s, and parts of the 2010s?

Rigorous independent research of some of the schools that began in this era found that they had a positive impact on their students compared with the schools that they replaced. Current data shows that, on average, the non-selective small schools created in the years this small booklet describes are getting their students to progress through their grades in a timely manner, earn passing scores on the necessary Regents exams (required of every student in New York State), and graduate on time about 83% of the time. This is a great achievement over the outcomes of the previous high school system.

One current group, the Performance Standards Consortium schools, has a different way of teaching and learning. They dispense for the most part with standardized testing and offer an alternative vision of student and school assessment. Their success in getting graduates into college—and the success of their students once they are in college—get much less attention than they deserve.

Charter schools came later to the high school sector and remain somewhat of a work in progress. Still, their students' exam scores are impressive, as are the rates their graduates get into college. These schools are clearly better than what existed in the past in the communities that these schools serve.

Metro IAF was present at the beginning of this important improvement in a critical public service, and it stayed involved in very tangible ways for as long as the city's mayor and school system leadership remained committed to sustaining these improvements. But elections have consequences, and upon Mayor Bill de Blasio's installation the school system moved sharply away from the things that had been working well. Thankfully, the new administration did not try to undo the good that had occurred in the city's high schools in the previous years, but it did cease to assess school performance, to close low-performing schools when warranted, and to encourage educators and community groups alike to design and support new effective schools. In addition, the state legislature of New York took a hostile turn on charter schools and the process of launching new charter schools in the city has largely ceased.

One of the challenges of organizing around education issues is that parenting school-age children is a particular phase of life. As their children grow up, parents naturally move on from schools being their central public concern to other, equally important, areas.

LESSONS FROM ONE CAMPAIGN

On the other hand, many young adults who are now leaders in the member institutions of Metro IAF were schoolchildren themselves when much of what I have described here occurred. By the later years of this story, we had a number of first-generation graduates from our new high schools now teaching in those schools. Time marches on, as they say, and the work of basic organizing—individual meetings, training, and issue identification—remains at the core of what effective community power organizations do. Building effective public relationships must always be intentional and focused on people and their self-interest, which is always changing and expanding. Tackling issues like educational reform follows this process; it does not lead it.

REFLECTIONS AND CONCLUSIONS

Community Organizing Can Help

Our school systems in the United States faces new and different challenges today than they did when we started this work in the 1990s. Many schools across the country now face the same challenges, including especially the disruption and loss of learning from the 2020 through 2022 school years due to the reduction or abandonment of in-person learning due to the Covid pandemic. The deep political divisions in our country, exacerbated by the tensions of the pandemic years, are also having a disruptive effect on schooling as arguments about what should be taught or read in school have taken a large toll on the respect due to educators and parents and the trust among all of us that is so necessary for schools to flourish. These arguments are often driven by forces far away from individual schools, often in the national media and on social media.

If one quote captured the political imagination of 2021, it was "Parents should not be able to tell schools what to teach," uttered by an unsuccessful candidate for governor in Virginia. He lost, partially because of that statement. Many parents were understandably angered by his arrogance, but that does *not* mean that parents should be able to tell schools what to teach. Effective schooling cannot occur when one side—parents or educators—hold all the power.

Effective schooling, like community organizing, is relational; it requires mutual respect and trust. That requires agreed-upon boundaries for what individual schools are going to emphasize in their curriculum and agreed-upon roles for both parents and educators in the joint effort of educating young people. For example, giving parents choice of schools—either within the school district or with independently run charter or private schools—can facilitate the process of aligning parental values and educational priorities; but once the choice is made, parents and educators need to be on the same page to make it work.

Today, the national debate about education is poisonous to those necessary school-family relationships. Educators feel set upon by sometimes unruly parents and are reverting to the defensive postures we found in the 1980s in New York City. Though it is hard to say exactly why, teacher resignations and retirements seem to be rising, with some saying they are "tired of being second-guessed."

This is not to say that parents are solely to blame. Again, because much of this debate is being fought nationally and anecdotes are becoming tweets and memes, some of the tension is coming as much from what teachers and parents are hearing about other locales as it is coming from what is going on in their own schools.

Educators must work to build support for what they are doing in schools. There is a clear role for schools to challenge their students to expand their

LESSONS FROM ONE CAMPAIGN

own horizons, but educators know that some topics, particularly related to human sexuality and gender, are sensitive areas for many parents. Bigotry, hatred, and denial of human nature can never be part of a public school's curriculum or practice, but discussions of the age-appropriateness of some lessons are, in my opinion, fair game for dialogue with parents. Again, trust is key. Parents need to be listened to as much as they need to be informed. When both parties are respectfully engaged in the dialogue, solutions are possible. Those discussions can happen best at a very local level, face to face. Left to the media, they get reduced to slogans and hateful caricatures.

The diverse, multi-faceted effort I witnessed and participated in to improve New York City's public high schools taught us that there is a time to fight the system, as we did in the late 1980s and 1990s, but such a fight must be undertaken in the spirit of improving the important institution of public education and not with an eye to destroying that institution. Only people who have a stake in the outcome can wage that type of fight. Partisan activists and central planners are sometimes loyal to their beliefs or theories, not to people. It is too easy for them to lose sight of what is important—the tangible and complex world of individuals working together daily for the benefit of those they cherish or for those they have chosen to serve professionally.

The Industrial Areas Foundation has, for over eighty years, understood and taught that their campaigns do not involve permanent friends or permanent enemies. In New York, the goal of our years of critiquing the school system was not to destroy it but to change the balance of power between those leading the system and those it was meant to serve. We needed to break down the barriers that the system had set up to keep communities and families at bay, and we needed to get the system to see parents, grandparents, and neighbors as individuals, not as representatives of various groups. When the political climate changed and we were able to work productively with the schools, including the design and creation of four new public high schools and two charter elementary schools, the years of developing local leaders and forging productive public relationships paid off in new ways.

LESSONS FROM ONE CAMPAIGN

Education is not easy, and neither is democracy. Both require active and informed participants. Both are a process, requiring give and take, challenge and compromise, and a willingness to find the best solution to a given local, tangible issue, not the perfect solution to a generalized, conceptual problem.

There is often a divide between professional educators and the families they serve. Individual parents often have a difficult time engaging with even the most well-intentioned professional educators. In the schools that Metro IAF designed, and in other new public schools created by others, the pastors and leaders of Metro's institutions were often able to bridge that divide. Because we had "skin in the game" having worked to create effective schools, local educators were able to trust our leaders. Well designed and respectful approaches to both the city's educational leadership and local school leaders were well-received, where they once had been stonewalled due to the pervasive mistrust that had existed between educators and parents. That work has continued even as Metro ceased to be involved in new school creation.

For more than twenty years, thousands of residents of New York City's poorer neighborhoods fought long and hard to get the schools that their children and grandchildren deserved, and they succeeded. They accomplished these things in ways that spoke directly to their own experiences in the schools and reflected the public relationships they had cultivated and maintained over the years. Even while decrying the state of their local schools, they forged lasting relationships with dedicated educators. They avoided attempted influences from the "experts" who viewed local issues from afar. Their story has much to offer to those who are seeking to improve local schools today in the face of an incredibly destructive bipartisan culture war over our nation's public schools.

BOOKS ON ORGANIZING AND LEADERSHIP

Bending Granite
30+ true stories of leading change
compiled by Tom Mosgaller, et. al.

Ed Marciniak's City and Church
A Voice of Conscience
by Charles Shanabruch

The Heartbeat of Wounded Knee
Native America from 1890 to Present
by David Treuer

Lessons Learned
Stories from a Lifetime in Organizing
by Arnie Graf

Reveille for a New Generation
Organizers and Leaders Reflect on Power
compiled by Gregory Pierce

Sometimes David Wins
Organizing to Overcome "Fated Outcomes"
by Frank C. Pierson, Jr.

Song in a Weary Throat
Memoir of an American Pilgrimage
by Pauli Murray

www.actapublications.com
800-397-2282